BEYBLADE™

Official Handbook

By J. MacKinnon

SCHOLASTIC INC.

New York Toronto London Auckland Sydney
Mexico City New Delhi Hong Kong Buenos Aires

ISBN 0-439-65355-X

Copyright © by HUDSON SOFT/TAKARA• BEYBLADE PROJECT• TV TOKYO. Licensed by d-rights Inc.

d-rights

All rights reserved. Published by Scholastic Inc., 557 Broadway, New York, NY 10012, by arrangement with Scholastic Canada, Ltd. SCHOLASTIC and associated logos are trademarks and/or registered trademarks of Scholastic Inc.

12 11 10 9 8 7 6 5 4 3 2   3 4 5 6 7 8/0

Printed in the U.S.A.   23

First printing, December 2003

A Brief Introduction by World Champion Beyblader Tyson

So you've discovered the sport of Beyblade and you're totally in love with it — you just can't get enough! Hey, I understand; I'm the current World Champion, and I love it just as much now as I did when I was an amateur, blading with the kids from my neighbourhood.

Yeah, that's right, I began blading in the streets with my friends — probably just like you. Hey, we've all got to start somewhere. It took a lot of hard work and practice to get where I am. Plus, I had tons of help from my Bit Beast, Dragoon, and my totally hype team, the Bladebreakers. With them behind me, I finally made it to the top. And, I gotta say, I like it here!

But enough about me, right? You're here to learn more about Beyblade, and you've come to the right place. My good friend Kenny is going to introduce you to the world's top Beybladers, so you'll know all of the key players, their Bit Beasts and their fighting styles. Then, I'm going to give you a rundown on what's happened so far, so you can see what it takes to be a world champion Beyblader. And, best of all, we're going to give you some amazing tips about the sport, so you can compete with the best.

And you never know, right? If you have the drive and the determination, you may just become the best. Well, maybe the second best — don't forget that I'm the World Champion, and I intend to keep it that way!

Anyway, I hope this Official Handbook totally helps you out in your game, but most of all, I hope that you have fun reading it, cause that's what Beyblading is really all about, right? So . . .

LET IT RIP!

— Tyson

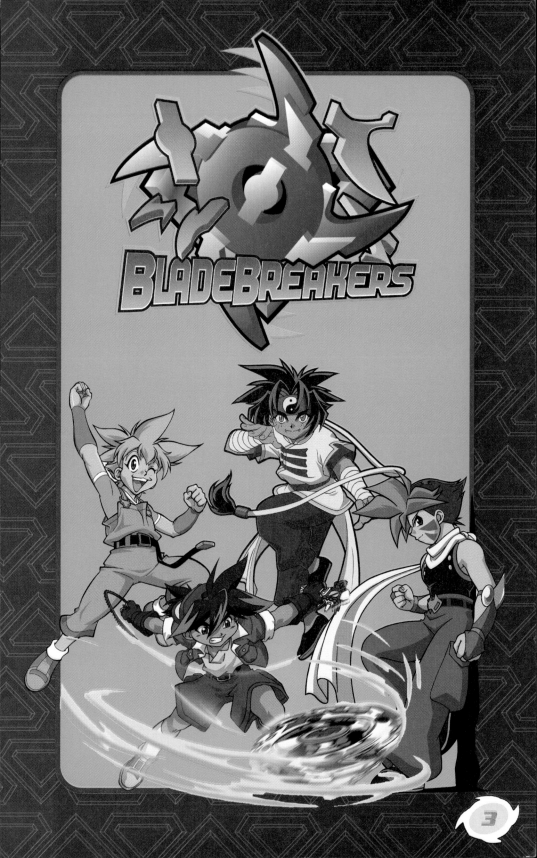

KENNY

Hi, I'm Kenny, otherwise known as "Chief." I may not be the best-known Bladebreaker, but I still like to think that Tyson, Max, Ray and Kai wouldn't have become World Champions without me.

Just like the rest of the Bladebreakers, I have a Bit Beast. Her name is Dizzara — or Dizzi for short. If a strange power surge hadn't trapped Dizzi in my laptop, maybe I could have become a world-class blader too. I guess I'll never know.

DIZZI

Even though Dizzi and I don't battle together, we still make a great team. Using all of the Beyblade data we collect, and scientific knowledge, we develop newer and more powerful blades. We also help our teammates with their training and strategy. We may not have all of the latest technology, but our Beyblade data obviously stands up against the best.

That's why I've been chosen to give you a rundown on some of today's best Beyblade teams, including the latest info on their attack styles and their Bit Beasts. I'll also tell you about some of the key players in the Beyblade world — not just the people on the teams, but the people behind the scenes who influence the sport more than we may have realized. Once you know who everyone is, you'll know almost as much about the sport as me and Dizzi!

I just hope my data's complete and I don't miss anything!

KAI

Beyblade: Dranzer Flame and Dranzer Spiral

Special Attacks: Fire Arrow, Flame Saber, and Spiral Survivor

Battle Style: Fierce and aggressive. Kai likes to get in there and take control right away.

Bit Beast: DRANZER

When we first met Kai, he was the leader of

the Blade Sharks, and, well, he was sort of scary. He and his teammates were battling kids and keeping their blades. That made Tyson really mad, so he took Kai on. Tyson lost, but he vowed to keep practicing until he could beat Kai.

I guess all the practicing paid off, because Tyson won his match against Kai at the Regional Qualifying Tournament! Even though he'd lost, Kai was made our team leader. Mr. Dickenson felt that Kai was a world-class blader, and that he could teach us a lot.

Kai did know a lot about Beyblading, but he was really mysterious, and we never knew what he was thinking. I guess you could say he was a loner, but once in a while, he would give us some great advice that totally helped out. He sure didn't like being on a team, though — all he wanted was to be the best and to do it all on his own.

Maybe that's why he was so drawn to Black Dranzer — the Beyblade created by the Biovolt Corporation to help it take over the world. Black Dranzer made Kai power-mad, and he fell right into the plans of Boris and Voltaire — Kai's evil grandfather! He even deserted us at the World Championships and joined the Demolition Boys. At least when the chips were down, Kai realized that he was being used and he needed us after all. He came back to the Bladebreakers and helped us take down Biovolt. He's one of the best bladers in the world, and we were really lucky to have him on our team.

Beyblade: Dragoon Grip Attacker, Dragoon Storm and Dragoon Phantom

Special Attacks: Vanishing Attack, Storm Attack and Phantom Hurricane

Battle Style: Very aggressive. Tyson plays more from the heart than from the head, but that doesn't mean he can't out-strategize his opponents.

Bit Beast: DRAGOON

People might think Tyson's too young and reckless to be a threat. They don't know how talented and determined he is.

He always stands up for what he believes in, and he's the best friend anyone could ask for — just don't try to come between him and a good all-you-can-eat buffet!

Tyson lives with his grandpa, who's totally into martial arts. He's the one who told Tyson about Dragoon, the Sacred Spirit of a dragon who existed in an ancient sword. When Tyson really needed help, Dragoon left the sword and became his Bit Beast. Together, Tyson and Dragoon are virtually unstoppable, and they get better with every match.

Tyson was still trying to earn his street cred when he heard about the Regional Qualifying Tournament. After he won that and became a Bladebreaker, he went on to win almost all of his tournament games. Without Tyson we never would have made it to the World Championships. Of course, while Tyson would be the first to agree with that, he would also be the first to add that the Bladebreakers never would have made it without Kai, Ray, Max or even me!

Oh, and before I forget, Tyson did something even more important — he saved the world. No one else could have defeated Tala, and that kept Boris and Voltaire from getting the Bit Beasts they needed to take over the world. So even though Tyson may seem like another in-your-face kid, just remember — the world owes him a lot!

RAY

Beyblade: Driger Slash and Driger Fang

Special Attacks: Tiger Claw and Tiger Fang

Battle Style: Calm and fearless. Ray thinks before he acts.

Bit Beast: DRIGER

We first met Ray at our Regional Qualifying Tournament when Mr. Dickenson brought him in as a challenger. At first Ray thought he was too good to have to compete against the likes of Tyson. Boy, was he ever surprised when Tyson beat him! Ray realized that Tyson was the superior blader, and bowed out of their tie-breaking third match. He had already decided he wanted to be part of our team.

Ray used to belong to the White Tigers, a group of Beybladers from a mountain village. His Bit Beast, Driger, came to him from Lee's grandfather, and had belonged to their tribe for as long as anyone could remember.

When we met the White Tigers we realized that they were going to be hard to beat. They were a tough team, we didn't have very much information about them and their desire to beat us was really personal. They were upset that Ray had left them. They didn't understand that Ray thought he could do more for himself, and his tribe, if he left home and learned all that he could.

Seeing the White Tigers again was really hard on Ray. When he lost a battle against his old teammate, Kevin, Driger left him! Ray thought he was nothing without his Bit Beast, and he almost went back to the White Tigers. He thought we wouldn't want him without Driger. In the end he came back to the Bladebreakers, and when he finally focused on winning the game, Driger came back!

Ray's a really levelheaded guy. He's quiet but confident, and his courage when he faced Bryan at the World Championships — beating him despite the odds — will probably go down in Beyblade history.

MAX

Beyblade: Draciel Metal Ball Defender, Draciel Shield and Draciel Fortress

Special Attacks: Metal Ball Defender, Wavegate and Fortress Defense

Battle Style: Max's strength lies in defense. He plans his moves and remains on the defensive until he sees his chance.

Bit Beast: DRACIEL

Max was the new kid in town when we met

him. He proved he was a talented blader when he managed to rescue a dog from drowning — using just his Beyblade!

At first I was a little jealous: He had great moves, his dad owned a shop that sold and repaired blades and he had his own Beystadium. But Tyson told me I couldn't be replaced, and I realized that Max was a pretty good guy to have as a friend.

The first time Max had help from Draciel was during the Regional Qualifying Tournament. He was battling Kai for a finalist position, and things weren't going very well. Suddenly, Max's blade flew at him, knocking a pendant that once had belonged to his grandmother from his neck. The pendant shattered, and when Max looked, he saw a strange piece of it lying on the ground. He tried it in his Beyblade, and it fit! Draciel emerged in the next round, and it was a wicked battle, even though Max didn't win.

One of Max's greatest achievements was when he won the American Tournament for us. To think we almost didn't let him play in the deciding round! But I guess he surprised a lot of people that day, including his mom.

Max is a really amazing guy to have around. He's always happy and full of energy. Even when things are at their worst, Max never lets anything get him down — he keeps our team spirit alive.

WHITE TIGERS

The White Tigers are one of the toughest teams out there. What they lack in technology, they make up for in sheer talent and ability. Defeating the White Tigers at the Asian Tournament was our first real challenge as a team. They wanted to smash us because they were so mad at Ray, but they managed to get over that. We actually get along with them pretty well now, which is a good thing.

I sure didn't enjoy being on their bad side!

LEE **Team Captain**

Special Attacks: Dark Lightning

Bit Beast:
GALEON

MARIAH

Special Attacks:

Scratch Attack,
Cat Bites

Bit Beast: GALUX

KEVIN

Special Attacks:

Crazy Monkey

Bit Beast: GALMAN

GARY

Special Attacks:

Bear Ax

Bit Beast: GALZZLY

ALL STARZ

The first time we met the All Starz was at their state-of-the-art training facility in America. They got us to battle them so they could study our moves. Of course, that gave us the same chance to study them. We soon knew that if we wanted to beat the All Starz — and all of the research and technology they had behind them — we had a lot of work to do. We worked hard and improved our skills and our blades. We also tried to make our moves less predictable — and it worked! It just goes to show that you can have the best of everything, but if you don't play with your heart, it really doesn't mean very much.

MICHAEL
Team Captain

Special Attacks:

Fastball

Bit Beast:

TRYGLE

EMILY

Special Attacks:

Water Smash

Bit Beast: TRYGATOR

EDDY

Special Attacks:

Sting Shoot

Bit Beast: TRYPIO

STEVE

Special Attacks:

Stampede Rush

Bit Beast: TRYHORN

MAJESTICS

We thought we'd seen it all, until we met the Majestics. When Tyson first battled Robert, we'd never seen a Bit Beast as big as Griffolyon! I was in a pretty big hurry to get to Russia for the World Championships, but Tyson knew that these European Beybladers could teach us a few things. We decided that we couldn't leave Europe without learning from the best. At first the Majestics just seemed to be spoiled rich kids. But they were superior players, and we lost to them several times before we finally took them down. Until they played against us, they'd never worked as a team before, and they just couldn't compete with the Bladebreakers when we all worked together. So they may have helped us improve our skills, but we taught them something about teamwork!

ROBERT
Team Captain

Special Attacks:

Wing Dagger

Bit Beast:
GRIFFOLYON

JOHNNY

Special Attacks:

Fire Rod

Bit Beast: SALAMALYON

ENRIQUE

Special Attacks:

Twin Destruction

Bit Beast: AMPHILYON

OLIVER

Special Attacks:

Earth Shake

Bit Beast: UNICOLYON

DEMOLITION BOYS

There's only one word you can use to describe the Demolition Boys — evil. Trained from an early age to feel nothing but hate and desire nothing but power, they are wickedly good Beybladers. They were trained by the Biovolt Corporation in a top-secret facility beneath an abbey in Russia. Boris and Voltaire, who run Biovolt, were using the boys to steal other bladers' Bit Beasts. Using the DNA of these Bit Beasts, they were artificially creating an army of new Bit Beasts so that they could take over the world. If the Bladebreakers hadn't defeated them at the World Championships, they might have succeeded!

TALA Team Captain

Special Attacks:

Blizzalog and Vinalog

Bit Beast:

WOLBORG

爆転シュート

IAN

Special Attacks:

Sand Bind

Bit Beast: WYBORG

SPENCER

Special Attacks:

Voda Impact and

Stramolyu

Bit Beast: SEABORG

BRYAN

Special Attacks:

Stroblitz

Bit Beast: FALBORG

don't forget . . .

So now you know all about the world's top Beybladers — but there are other, less well-known, people who've had a real influence on the sport. Without some of these people, the Bladebreakers might not have won the World Championship. And without some of the others . . . well, we might have won much more easily!

Stanley A. Dickenson

Mr. Dickenson is the Chairman of the BBA (Beyblade Battle Association). His organization promotes and trains the world's top Beybladers. That makes him the most important man in the sport. Mr. Dickenson also brought the Bladebreakers together — we were part of his plan to defeat the Demolition Boys and stop Biovolt.

Dr. Judy Tate

Judy is Max's mom and Head Director of the American BBA. She's in charge of Project: Power Beyblade, and her research facilities are heavily funded by the American government — they're even considered a matter of national security! They have all of the latest technology — there are computers everywhere! If I had that technology at my fingertips, we'd be unstoppable! Judy is also responsible for training the All Starz and providing them with state-of-the-art equipment.

DJ Jazzman, Brad Best and A.J. Topper

A Beyblade tournament is nothing if these guys aren't
there to commentate and pump up the crowd! Brad and
A.J. are always joking, and Jazzman is a total bolt of
energy — the perfect person to get bladers hyped before
their match!

Grandpa Granger

He's a hip-hop granddaddy to his g-son, Tyson —
and Tyson couldn't be more embarrassed. We all love
Grandpa, even if we don't always understand him . . .
He tries a little too hard to be hip, I guess. But he's an
amazing grandfather, and a talented martial arts master.
He has the power and agility of someone half his age. I
think he'd always hoped that he could train Tyson in the
martial arts, but he's still behind Tyson's Beyblading
100%. He's one of our team's biggest fans!

Tyson's Dad

Tyson thought his dad was away on an archaeological dig — he never dreamed that his own father had been hired by the BBA to uncover the mystery of Bit Beasts! Tyson's dad discovered that Bit Beasts, or Sacred Spirits, have existed alongside humans since the dawn of civilization. Some of these Bit Beasts remain in hibernation, and Tyson's dad is trying to find one of these creatures so he can unlock the mystery of their beginnings.

Mr. Tate

Mr. Tate is Max's dad, and he's really helped us out a lot. He owns his own hobby shop where he sells and repairs Beyblades. He's also one of our biggest supporters, and we've really benefited from his experience — especially when he helped build Tyson's superpowered blade for the World Championships!

Voltaire

Voltaire is president of the Biovolt Corporation, one of the world's largest companies. He's also Kai's grandfather and a criminal mastermind! Ever since Kai was a kid, his grandfather has used him in his evil plots. He wanted Kai to steal Bit Beasts for him and help him take over the world! We were really relieved when Kai proved he wanted nothing more to do with his grandfather.

Boris Balkov

Boris is Voltaire's henchman and he's in charge of Balkov Abbey. Boris oversaw all of the experiments on Bit Beasts, and he was using Bit Beast DNA to make Bit Beasts for his own evil purposes. He was even responsible for brainwashing the kids they were training! Boris brought together the Demolition Boys and trained them until they were more machine than human. He was also in on Voltaire's plan to take over the world. Boris is a really nasty guy, and I hope he pays for what he did!

The Dark Bladers

The Dark Bladers offered us our first clue that there was more to Beyblading and Bit Beasts than we'd realized! At first we thought these creepy guys were totally evil — they were bent on stealing our Bit Beasts! According to my files, they'd each been beaten by a member of the Majestics, and they felt humiliated. They vowed to take all of the Bit Beasts in the world so that no one would ever be able to beat them again. They came together to plot their revenge, and the dark skies gave them the power to get it. But once we beat the Majestics, their curse was lifted — they no longer had to steal Bit Beasts. I *guess* they're sort of our friends now . . .

EPISODE GUIDE

Hi, Tyson with you again! Kenny was going to tell you
about everything that happened to us on the way to
the World Championships, but I told him that it was my
turn. If I forget anything, he'll let me know — trust me.
He won't let me leave out anything important, and I
won't let him put in anything boring!

   I guess it all began when I met Kenny for the first
time and had that run-in with Carlos from the Blade
Sharks . . .

1 The Blade Raider

I was supposed to meet Andrew for a Beybattle, but first I had to escape Grandpa — *not easy!* When I finally got to Andrew, Carlos was challenging him. Carlos said whoever lost to him had to give him their blade. I was so mad I told him I'd take him on right then and there. That's when I met Kenny. He stopped me and told me my blade had to be way faster to beat Carlos. With hard work, and help from my friends, I improved my blade and went looking for Carlos. He didn't stand a chance — I took him down in no time. I told him he had to give back all of the blades he'd taken. That's when Kai showed up.

2 Day of the Dragoon

So Kai and I battled, and he won — big deal. That just meant I had more practicing to do. Back then Kai led the Blade Sharks, and he was looking for the ultimate Bit Beast. Of course, that made Kenny's data pretty important, so they kidnapped him and Dizzi! I decided to ask the spirit of Dragoon for help. I never thought he'd leave the ancient sword he was in and enter my Beyblade — but I was happy he did! When I found Kenny, I challenged Kai to let him go. This time the battle was more evenly matched, thanks to Dragoon. We tied, but at least Kenny was free.

3 Take It to the Max!

This is when we met Max, and Kenny already told you how it happened. But he didn't tell you that Max and I battled — in his very own Beystadium! He beat me, but he promised to teach me some of his moves. Just as we were about to go again, Mr. Dickenson showed up and told us about the Regional Qualifying Tournament. Max, Kenny and I agreed to practice for it together. Kenny told me that I had a lot of work to do. I didn't want to hear that, and I guess I said some really mean things. I apologized, and Kenny forgave me — especially when he saw me practice my awesome new moves!

4 The Qualifier Begins

The Regional Qualifying Tournament was wild! At first we competed in blocks, so a group of us would battle at the same time, and the last one standing won. Kai won Block A, and Max won Block B. Kenny competed in Block C, and he would have won, if Kai hadn't butted in. Then I was up in Block D — along with four of the Blade Sharks. They might have taken me out, but Carlos turned on his own team! After he'd defeated them, he came after me. That's when I called in my secret weapon — it made my blade so fast, it became *invisible*. Carlos sure didn't see it coming, and I won Block D!

5 A Draciel of Approval

The Semi-Finals opened with Max versus Kai in the Tower Dish for a best-of-three round. Max almost took the first battle, but Kai used his Spin Fire Attack and knocked him out. In the next battle, Max tried a reverse launch, and the backspin helped him boot Kai from the tower! Then something crazy happened — Max's Beyblade flew at the pendant he was wearing and smashed it! A piece fell from the pendant, so Max tried it in his Beyblade. *It fit!* The last battle was fierce, and everyone was shocked when Draciel flew from Max's blade. Unfortunately, even though Draciel was amazing, he wasn't a match for Dranzer. Kai was still undefeated.

6 Dragoon Storm

It was the last round of the Semi-Finals, and I was up against Ray — an undefeated champion brought in by Mr. Dickenson. In the very first battle, Ray totally shattered my blade. Just as I was about to be disqualified because I couldn't fix it, Kenny came to the rescue! He fixed my blade, and he added the new defensive ring that he and Dizzi had designed. When Ray tried his Tiger Claw Attack again, I countered with my Storm Attack — my blade was spinning so fast, it created a tornado! Driger and Dragoon fought it out, and Dragoon won! Ray forfeited the third battle — he said that I was the better player.

7 Thirteen Candles

Okay, so this is how hard I was practicing for the Finals: *I forgot my own birthday!* Grandpa threw me a party, but then I had to face Kai in our first of three battles. Being 13 must suit me, because I took Kai out in the first battle. He had me in the second battle with his Fire Arrow Attack. The third battle was *intense*. We both brought out our Bit Beasts right away, and storm met fire with a clash. Storm won out, and I was the winner of the National Beyblade Tournament! That's when Mr. Dickenson announced the National Team: Me, Max, Ray and our new team captain, Kai.

8 Bladin' in the Street

So our new team was off to the Asian Qualifier, and Kenny got to go too! On the flight over, he gave me his latest design: the Catapult Grip Shooter. It was totally rad! We had a stopover in Hong Kong and ran into some trouble. This kid Bruce chal- lenged us to a street match, and I decided to take him on. It was time to earn my street cred. Bruce was a strong player, but once Dragoon came out, it was game over. That's when Kevin from the White Tigers appeared. He'd totally used Bruce to spy on us and see our bit power before the Asian Qualifier!

9 Showdown in Hong Kong

It turned out that Ray used to be a White Tiger, and he knew Kevin. I decided to teach Kevin a lesson and we battled — *in a wok!* He won the first battle with his Crazy Monkey Attack, but my Storm Attack took him out in the second battle. That's when the rest of the White Tigers showed up. They were angry at Kevin for spying, but they were also mad at Ray. They called him a traitor, but it seemed like they still wanted him on the White Tigers. That made Kai angry and he challenged their leader, Lee, to a match. Lee decided to save it for the tournament, but Mariah was ready to take Kai on. For some reason, he refused.

10 Battle in the Sky

I was on top of the world at the Asian Tournament — literally! China Tower is really high above the mountains! Our first match was against the Tall Boys. We battled it out in an intense dish that was designed like a mountain range. Ray was up first against Andre and his Yak Bit Beast. Ray almost knocked himself out of the dish, but he recovered for the win. Next, Max defeated Waylan — despite the heat wave Waylan sent out. Then it was me against Tommy. He used his Muay Thai Kick, and it looked bad for me for a while, but I washed him out with a wave. And that was it — the Bladebreakers were on to the next round!

11 Bye Bye Bit Beast

Kenny was up late working out a way for us to beat the White Tigers. He left to get some tea, and Kevin came in, stole his data and put it on a disk! Ray stopped Kevin, and they battled. Ray was winning, but when Kevin begged him for mercy, Ray hesitated to finish him off. That's when Driger disappeared! Kevin knew that if Ray played half-heartedly, he would lose Driger. That's what Kevin had been counting on. He won the match; then I battled him and got the disk back. Kevin didn't care — he'd hurt Ray, and that was all he'd wanted. He thought it would earn him Lee's respect.

12 Adios Bladebreakers

Ray left the tournament because he thought he was worthless without Driger. Max and I went looking for him, but Mariah found him first. When we showed up, she had almost convinced him to return to the White Tigers! Max and I were *not* happy. I challenged Ray, and said that if *I* won he had to stick with the Bladebreakers; if *he* won, he could do what he wanted. I still can't believe it, but Ray beat me without a Bit Beast! Mariah had reminded him that he was still a good blader, even without Driger. So he was free to chose the White Tigers . . . but he still chose the Bladebreakers!

13 Crouching Lion, Hidden Tiger

The White Tigers had won their most recent round against the Spin Shepherds 2–1, and it seemed more and more certain that we would be facing them in the Finals. We went up against the Charming Princes and won all three of our battles. We were happy to win so easily, but even better — Driger came back! Ray's determination to beat Robin from the Charming Princes was so strong, that Driger returned!

14 The Race Is On

It was the day of the Semi-Finals, and I guess I slept in a bit. The others went on to the tournament, but Ray waited for me and we caught a later bus. We would have been okay, but then a landslide blocked traffic. So we began climbing the mountain to China Tower. It sure wasn't easy — especially when Ray got hurt and I had to carry him! At the tournament, Max had won against Chucky Chunk from the Blade Hunters, and Kai had beaten Zippy. So I was up next — only I wasn't there! With seconds left before we had to forfeit the match, Ray and I made it. I won my round, and the Bladebreakers were going on to the Finals!

15 Going for the Gold

So we finally went head-to-head against the White Tigers for the Asian Championship. First it was Max against Gary and his Bear Ax Attack. Max wore Gary down and won the first battle. But Gary got way more focused and tore up the dish in the second and third battles to take Max out. Next it was Ray versus Mariah. They have some serious history, so we knew that it wasn't going to be easy for Ray.

16 My Enemy, My Friend

Mariah and Ray battled in the Forbidden City dish, and Mariah won the first match. It seemed like Ray was taking it easy on her, so she demanded that he try harder. Kai also had a few words with him. Ray finally got it, and Driger's Tiger Claw Attack defeated Galux's Scratch Attack in the second battle. The third match was fierce, and the crowd went wild. They loved Mariah and Ray! During the battle Driger and Galux created a bond to help fix Ray and Mariah's friendship, and it worked! They vowed to be friends no matter what. Then Ray went in for the kill. So the Finals were tied and I was up next!

17 A Score to Settle

Before my match against Lee, Kenny gave me a new shooter to help my blade manoeuvre in the Desert Temple Dish. Lee won our first battle with his Dark Lightning Attack. In the next battle I whipped up a funnel cloud and blew Lee away. The third battle we both fell out of the dish at the same time — for a *tie!* Ray took on Lee for the tiebreaker, and was it ever personal! Ray used his Tiger Claw Attack, and Lee retaliated with *Gary's* Bear Ax! Ray turned the tables on him by using a twist on Dark Lightning. He took out the dish and Lee's blade with it! The Bladebreakers had won the Asian Tournament!

18 A Star Is Born

Hot out of the Asian Championship, we went home and found out we were famous! My new celebrity sort of went to my head, and I neglected my blade. I even left it behind when I went out to greet my new fans. Too bad nobody believed I was me! I saw this bully named Riley destroy another kid's blade. The kid, Nicky, was really upset, so I took him to Max's and we made his blade better than new. Nicky was so happy, and that made me realize how stupid I'd been. Then it was payback time. With his new blade, Nicky destroyed Riley's blade, but when he saw that Riley had learned his lesson, Nicky offered to help fix it.

19 Under the Microscope

Soon we were in America where we toured one of the world's most advanced BBA research facilities. The technology was impressive, but we were in for a shock — especially Max. We found out that his mother, Judy, was Head Director of the American BBA! Max had thought she worked at a *college*. When I said that a Beyblade is only as powerful as the person who uses it, Judy's assistant, Emily, challenged us. Ray and I won our matches against Tony and Andy, but Emily crushed Max. We found out we'd been tricked, and that they had only battled us to determine our skill level! Judy was pretty confident that her team, the All Starz, could beat us.

20 It's All Relative

Max was really upset that he'd lost to Emily, especially in front of his mom. We decided we needed to learn more about the facility, so we took a little "self-guided" tour. The place had everything: battle simulators, virtual-reality training gear, a top-of-the-line computer network and a sports complex. The All Starz even had their Bit Beasts developed in a lab! It just didn't seem right. Then these two guys, Steve and Eddy, came out of nowhere. Their trash talk really got under Ray's skin, so he challenged Steve to a Beybattle. Steve won, but at least we'd learned more about them.

21 Practice Makes Perfect

We didn't mind Mr. Dickenson sending us off to a training camp — until we got there and saw that it was a shack in the middle of nowhere. Nobody was there except for this kid named Antonio. He said he would train us, but he could hardly launch his own blade! I said I'd help him, but the others thought I should practice instead. Kenny and Ray reconfigured Driger for the American Tournament while the others trained. The next day Antonio challenged me again, and he won! Kai had thought I needed to learn something, so he'd told Antonio how to beat me.

22 Blading With the Stars!

Before the American Tournament there was a celebrity match in Tippecanoe. Max, Emily and Spintensity's Mario faced off against an actress, a boxer and the mayor. The winner would be the team with the most surviving blades. Emily wanted to prove she was the best — she took out the celebrity team to win the first battle! She refused to work with her team. In the next battle Max collided with Emily and that left her as a target for the celebrities. He and Mario were wiped out too, and the celebrities won. The last battle was the tiebreaker, and Emily wasn't doing so well. Max helped her and Mario out and they won!

23 Showdown in Vegas

As the American Tournament began in Las Vegas's Glitter Dome, we learned that the All Starz's Beyblades automatically transmit and receive new information. I wasn't worried — Kenny had updated my blade and it was wicked! I called it Phantom Dragoon. We were up against the Renegades, and Kai decided to battle. He wanted to confuse Emily and her data. He took on Miguel and his Battle Ballad Attack in a miniature Grand Canyon dish, and he easily won. Next Max took out Pedro the Matador to win his match. Then I was up against José and his Rapid Fire Attack. Of course, José didn't stand a chance against my Dragoon Phantom Hurricane Attack, and we were on to the next round!

24 Viva Las Vegas

Next we were up against the Savage Slammers in the Tsunami Beystadium. Ray and his tricked-out new blade went head-to-head with Diego and his Iguana Attack. At first it looked like Diego was doing nothing, but when Ray least expected it, the Iguana rose up and sent a wave that crushed him. Next up, Max versus Fernando and his Seal Shark Attack. Fernando and his blade were no match for Draciel, though, and Max took the second round. Then I battled it out with Axl and his Tortoise Grenade. Axl, or as I like to call him, Turtle Boy, was driving me crazy, but eventually I focused and washed him out with my Phantom Hurricane Attack.

25 My Way or the Highway

I'm sort of embarrassed about the Semi-Finals. I guess I'd overdone it at the buffet the night before, and I wasn't feeling too good. That meant Kai had to substitute for me against Spintensity. First Max battled against Luiz and his Dancing Crash Attack in the New Jersey Turnpike dish. Once Max figured out Luiz's rhythm, he had him beat. Next Ray went up against Frankie. When she called on her Marine Decoy Attack, her blade morphed into a school of Beyblade-eating piranha! But when Driger vanished and then attacked her from behind, Ray took the win. Mario didn't stand a chance against Kai — it was over in seconds. We'd made it to the Finals!

26 Catch a Shooting All Star

Kenny told Max he couldn't play in the Finals because the All Starz already knew all his moves. Max was not happy — he'd wanted to win in front of his mom. He left our room and ran into Judy, who upset him even more. She said that all of her data predicted that he would lose against her team. Max asked Kenny again if he could compete, and Kai said we should let him. In the first round of the Finals, I took on Steve. I easily won our first battle, but I think Steve let me so they could analyze my moves. Why do I think that? Because Tryhorn totally smashed me in the second battle!

27 The Battle of America

Before our third battle, Dizzi said that there was no way I could beat Steve — he was just too powerful. He knew all my moves, so I came up with new strategy as I went. He started getting really steamed, especially when I surprised him from behind. He came after me again, and Kai said to let him hit me and absorb his energy. It worked! I unleashed my Phantom Hurricane, and that was the end of Steve. Next, Ray was up against Eddy in the Satellite Dish II. Eddy used his basketball moves and Scorpio to take Ray out in two rounds. The Finals were tied — it was all up to Max. He freaked, but we convinced him he could do it.

28 Bottom of the 9th

Max faced Michael in the Field of Doom dish, and Michael took the first battle. I told Max to think more with his heart and less with his head, and he won the next one! The All Starz couldn't believe it. In the third battle, Michael threw a blazing fastball. Max realized that if he couldn't match Michael's power, he could use it against him. He forced Michael to use more and more energy until it shorted out the All Starz's entire system! Max won! Even though he'd proved her wrong, Judy was really proud of him. So were we — the Bladebreakers were headed for the World Championships!

29 Play it Again Dizzi

Now that we were on our way to the World Beyblade Championships in Russia, the Chief thought he should review everything that had happened so far. He figured that if he analyzed all of our moves, then he could see our strengths, and where we needed to improve. When he was done, we had a surprise in store for him — we boarded a cruise ship bound for Russia!

30 Cruising for a Bruising

I don't think Kenny enjoyed the cruise. He was seasick, and all he wanted to do was develop a new training regime so we'd be ready for Russia. While I was out on my run, I happened to go by the games room and see this bully, Robert, battling some kids and busting up their blades. I challenged him, and when I called out Dragoon, he called out Griffolyon — the biggest Bit Beast I'd ever seen. His blade spun so fast, it created a storm that blew me off my feet! I felt like such a loser until Kai gave me some good advice. I vowed to practice more and be better prepared next time.

31 London Calling

Our ship left us behind in England! Kenny wanted to catch a plane to Russia, but I knew that if we took a train, we could learn from the European bladers. Before we left London, a videotape mysteriously arrived. My *dad* was on it — talking about Bit Beasts! Later this creepy guy, Cenotaph, snatched my blade, so we chased him. When we caught up, his mummy Bit Beast, Sarcopholon, was trying to take Dragoon. Ray and Max sent Driger and Draciel in to help, but it was a trap! If Kai's Fire Arrow Attack hadn't set the mummy on fire, who knows what would have happened!

32 Darkness at the End of the Tunnel

We were on a train watching a monster movie when the Dark Bladers appeared and challenged us! Cenotaph grabbed Kenny, so we had to agree to a battle. They told us that if we lost, they'd turn our Bit Beasts into Dark Creatures! I took on Sanguinex. His Drac-Attack was mean, but I was gaining the edge — until he threw another blade in! Next Max and Lupinex jumped in. We were in trouble until we saw that the Dark Bladers' Bit Beasts were the monsters from the movie. Max and I used the Vampire Vamoose Attack to finish Sanguinex. Using a silver dollar on his blade, Ray took Lupinex out. Lucky for us, help arrived before Zomb and Cenotaph could get into it!

33 Last Tangle in Paris

There we were in Paris, and, as usual, Kai was missing. We were at the Eiffel Tower looking for him when the Dark Bladers showed up. They demanded our Bit Beasts, so Ray asked why they wanted them. They told us a *long* story about how they'd lost battles because they hadn't had Bit Beasts, so they'd vowed to take everyone else's. *Anyway* . . . we battled them. Sarcopholon and Zomb's Shamblor were powerful, and Lupinex and Sanguinex almost finished us off! We were about to give up when Kai showed up with his tricked-out new blade, and we beat them! Once they were gone, we met Oliver.

34 Art Attack

Kenny dragged me off to the Louvre. I wasn't really into it, but I was still totally angry when I found out that Oliver had rented it and it was closed! I sneaked in and told Oliver off, and he offered to cook me lunch — he's some big-deal chef in Paris. It was the best meal ever, but when he said I didn't know how to control Dragoon, I challenged him. His Unicolyon was even bigger than Griffolyon, but I used his power against him, and we tied. Oliver suggested that we go to Italy next and look up Enrique.

35 When in Rome, Beyblade!

So we went looking for Enrique in Rome, but he sure wasn't what we expected. He wouldn't agree to battle — until I called him a chicken. We went head-to-head in his very own Beystadium, based on the Coliseum. Enrique came out to battle dressed like a gladiator, and he used a sword winder. His Bit Beast Amphilyon had two heads and his blade could double for the attack! Once he'd defeated Dragoon, Amphilyon came at *me*. If Dragoon hadn't come between us, I don't know what would have happened. Kenny was really mad, so Enrique offered me a rematch.

36 Déjà Vu All Over Again

I was still upset that Enrique had beat me — I'd thought I was the best. The guys helped me improve my gear spin ratio, and after some pizza, we came up with a blade that was less predictable. I was practicing when Enrique showed up with Oliver. The rematch was on! Enrique actually threatened to *punish* Amphilyon if he didn't win! Dragoon tricked Amphilyon so that his two heads attacked each other. I started to win, so Enrique threatened his Bit Beast again. That's when Amphilyon attacked *him!* Dragoon took a real beating trying to protect Enrique, but he finally stopped Amphilyon. Even though I'd won, Enrique said I wasn't anything special until I could beat Robert.

37 A Knight to Remember

Oliver took us to Robert's castle in his hot air balloon. Robert kept us waiting forever, and when I couldn't wait anymore, I went looking for him. I guess I got a *little* lost. Suddenly, I fell through a trap door! Then I was attacked by *walls*, dropped into a tunnel and came out in a fireplace — with fire in it! That's where I finally found Robert, Johnny and the others. I demanded a rematch, but Robert said I wasn't up to his high standards! Johnny made us a deal — if we could beat him, we could fight Robert. He took on Kai and their battle was *vicious.* Kai tried his Flame Thrower Attack, but then Salamalyon came out. Even Kai looked scared! He did his best, but Johnny won.

38 Olympia Challenge

We challenged Robert and his friends as a team, and refused to leave until they accepted. They'd never fought as a team before, but they agreed on one condition — if they won, they would take our place in Russia! We were freaked when the Dark Bladers showed up, but they said if we defeated their enemies, they'd be freed from their curse. Ray and Oliver were up first. They knocked each other out at the exact same time, so the score was tied.

39 A Majestic Battle . . . A Majestic Victory

Next Kai and Johnny were up. Kai came out strong, but Johnny began to get the best of him. We tried to help, but Kai said to leave him alone. There was no chance of that — I wanted to win. I told him to try the same move Dragoon had used to get away from Amphilyon in Rome. Kai told Dranzer to fly, and it worked! Kai won, but he was still mad. Then I finally had my shot at Robert. He used his Wing Dagger Attack, but Dragoon and I took him down! We had avenged ourselves and the Dark Bladers. Later we ran into Mr. Dickenson and found out he'd *planned* for all this to happen!

40 Hot Battle in a Cold Town

Finally we were in Russia. *Man* was it ever cold! We were checking out Moscow when we ran into Boris, who invited us to lunch. I can't believe I ate with him! Then he showed us around his training facility. I wasn't too impressed, so Boris said I should challenge one of his trainees. I went up against this kid, Alexander, whose shooter looked like some kind of anchor. He was killing me, but then Kai gave me a great idea. I came down hard on Alexander's blade and my Phantom Hurricane Attack took him out. He couldn't believe he'd lost. *I* couldn't believe Boris kicked him out of the program!

41 Out of the Past

Something weird was going on with Kai, but we didn't really know it at the time. He was having all of these flashbacks, so he went to Balkov Abbey to get some answers. What he saw was totally messed up. The rest of us were checking out Moscow's street action, and we ran into the White Tigers and the All Starz. Emily and Mariah did *not* hit it off, and their teams decided to battle for fun. Steve was up first against Mariah. He called out Tryhorn, but Mariah and Galux took him out. Next Emily defeated Gary. Then Michael and Lee went head-to-head, which was awesome! They were both such fierce players that it ended in a tie.

42 Drawn to the Darkness

Kai told us later what had happened, but all we knew then was that he was missing. He was still at the abbey, and he suddenly realized that he'd grown up there! Boris appeared and asked him to join Biovolt (Beybladers Intent On Victory Over Lawless Tyranny) and help it take over the world. Kai refused and took off, but Boris followed him with the security cameras. He had Kai attacked; he even used fiery Beyblades, but Kai escaped. Then Kai found Black Dranzer and remembered everything — being a kid and seeing Black Dranzer and wanting its power. He'd taken the blade, but he couldn't control it, and it had nearly destroyed the abbey. Kai had been so traumatized, he'd forgotten everything — until then. Boris asked him again to join Biovolt, and when he offered him Black Dranzer, Kai couldn't resist.

43 Live and Let Kai

Still no sign of Kai, and we were worried. We decided to go to Biovolt Beystadium to watch the All Starz take on the Demolition Boys. Steve, whose blade was loaded with attack rings, was up against Ian, but he couldn't beat his reverse slam. Next Eddy went head-to-head with Tala and he lost too. Then the Demolition Boys' surprise blader came out — *and it was Kai!* We couldn't believe it! Kai took on all of the All Starz at once, and even as a team they couldn't beat him and his Black Dranzer Fire Attack. But the absolute worst part was when Kai let Black Dranzer absorb all of the All Starz's Bit Beasts!

44 Losing Kai

Next Kai destroyed the White Tigers using the All Starz's stolen Bit Beasts. Then he took Galzzly, Galux and Galeon too! After the match we went looking for him at the abbey. While Kenny, Max and Ray kept the kids who were chasing us busy, I looked for Kai. Boris found me first. He and I were in a lab they used for concentrating the fighting spirit of the Bit Beasts. Boris told me all about Kai's past, and how with Kai's help, Biovolt would rule the world. He also showed me how Kai was using a simulator to determine the best way to destroy the Bladebreakers! When I finally saw Kai in person, he threw Dranzer at my feet and said he didn't need us.

45 Breaking the Ice

Max was at the airport seeing his mom off, but the rest of us were taken to meet Kai on a frozen lake. We battled hard, but Kai quickly took us down. At the airport, Judy gave Max a tricked-out new blade. When Emily ran up and showed him a satellite photo of us, he knew we were in trouble. Judy gave him a lift in her plane, and just as Kai was about to take our Bit Beasts, Max parachuted in! His new blade actually deflected Black Dranzer. Then I threw in a very upset Dranzer, and Kai lost! Suddenly the ice cracked — Kai was sinking on an ice floe! We managed to save him, and Kai realized he needed us after all!

46 First Strike

Okay, so right here is where we learned a whole lot of stuff about our Bit Beasts and the Biovolt Corporation. So this part is going to be a lot bigger, but it's all important stuff. Pay attention!

Kai went to the abbey to give back Black Dranzer. When he returned he told us that Biovolt recruited kids who thought they were being trained to become Beybladers. Instead, they were being brainwashed into ruthless warriors to help Biovolt take over the world. Boris was also creating Bit Beasts from Bit Beast DNA. The man-made creatures were placed into Beyblades, and then sent out to capture and merge with real Bit Beasts. Only the strongest Beybladers could control these creatures, and that's where the Demolition Boys came in.

As Kai was telling us this, Mr. Dickenson and Grandpa showed up! *With my dad!* We found out that the Bladebreakers were part of a BBA plan to stop Biovolt, and that Mr. Dickenson had hired my dad to do an archaeological study on Bit Beasts. It turns out Bit Beasts are as old as the Earth itself, and they placed their life-essence into objects of great power so they could remain hidden until they were needed. Many are still in hibernation, and my dad was trying to find artifacts that contained these creatures. He was close to making an important discovery when Boris showed up and started asking questions.

The police contacted my dad and said that Boris was a criminal mastermind, and that he might be working with Voltaire, the head of the Biovolt Corporation.

My dad told Mr. Dickenson about the talk he'd had with the police, but the BBA had already been watching Biovolt for a while. They were convinced Voltaire was plotting to take over the world by sending out an army of powerful Bit Beasts created for war. That's when Kai told us that Voltaire was his grandfather! Man, and I'd thought *Grandpa* was bad! After hearing all of this, we knew the Bladebreakers had to stop the Demolition Boys before it was too late.

We were on the BBA bus later when a helicopter forced us off the road. It landed on the bus's roof, and Ian jumped out! Max took him on, and Draciel and Wyborg came out and collided. When Ian's blade landed back in his hand, we thought it was over, but then two more blades came at us. All of the Demolition Boys had arrived, and Max took them on alone. Spencer called out Seaborg and his Tidal Wave Attack, and Max and his blade were both knocked down. Max's leg was hurt, but worse than that, Spencer's blade sucked up Draciel!

47 A Lesson for Tyson

Things looked bad — Max was hurt, and we were frozen and stranded in the middle of nowhere. Then a bus came along — Oliver and Enrique were on it! They took us to an old castle, and Robert and Johnny were there. Robert said he wanted to take the Bladebreakers down. Robert and I battled, and he kept winning. Then he said that instead of getting mad and wasting it on words, I had to channel it into my blade. I directed my energy into Dragoon. We battled again, and it worked! Dragoon took Griffolyon down. Then we found out that Mr. Dickenson had hired the Majestics to teach us a lesson!

48 Victory in Defeat

The World Championships, and Kai was up first against Spencer in the Black Sea bowl. Kai was holding his own until Spencer set loose his Voda Impact, and Kai's blade was chased by a tsunami! Kai tried his Flame Saber Attack, but Seaborg put out his flame, and soon it was all over. Kai took off after he lost, and when he came back he was acting strange. We saw Black Dranzer in his hand and were worried, but Kai betrayed Voltaire and called out Dranzer in the second battle. He knew he couldn't win, but since he had us, he wasn't afraid to lose. Spencer took the match — and then he took Dranzer.

49 A Wicked Wind Blows

Next up: Ray versus Bryan in the RPM dish. Bryan won the first battle after he injured Ray. They battled again and Ray released Driger with a vengeance. Bryan called on Falborg, and his Stroblitz Attack turned the *air* into a weapon that struck Ray again and again. We told Ray to call it off, but he wouldn't! It turned out that Bryan had no defense, and Ray took him out with his Tiger Claw. Ray was totally out of it in the last match, and Driger had to shield him from Bryan. But suddenly Ray came back! He called out his Tiger Claw Attack, and it knocked Bryan down and his blade out. Ray won, but he had to be wheeled out on a stretcher.

50 New and Cyber Improved

Max's mom and dad, Kenny, Max and Emily built me Super Dragoon — the world's first superpowered blade! While they were doing that, I was practicing with Kai. Michael, Lee and, Robert showed up, too, and gave me a real workout! Soon it was time for the match: me and Dragoon versus Tala and Wolborg in the Blizzard Bowl. The battle was fierce — Tala was using my friends' moves against me! I was pretty freaked, but everyone reminded me that their Bit Beasts didn't like Tala. I managed to take the first battle, but Tala said he'd let me. The next battle, though, was out of this world. Literally.

53

51 Final Showdown

I didn't know where I was, or what was going on — Biovolt Beystadium was gone and Tala and I were alone. Tala told me that when our Bit Beasts collided, they had fractured the space-time continuum, and we'd warped to another dimension! It seemed like I was in a blizzard, but everyone in the Beystadium could still see us — we were inside an iceberg! Our second battle was still on, and I released Dragoon. Then Tala released every single Bit Beast he'd captured over the years — including some of my friends. I was so cold, I couldn't stop shivering, and it was hard to focus on the match. Tala won when he knocked me and Dragoon down. We were totally tied, so everything depended on our final battle. I guess most people thought that it was all over for me, but something happened and I was back in the game!

I'd realized that even though Tala had a stronger blade, blading was all about passion and that was my strength. Tala tried his Wolborg Ultimate Attack and all of the Bit Beasts under his control merged into the ultimate fighting weapon — a huge fireball! It started to head for me, but it didn't take me out! I brought on Dragoon, and he spoke to me! He told me that as long as I believed in him, he'd never leave! It was so wicked! Then I called on his Final Attack! The battle was unbelievable! Dragoon managed to penetrate the ball of fire and the force of it burst the iceberg! I was free, everyone got their Bit Beasts back, and Tala's blade was no longer spinning. I'd won! Biovolt was defeated, and the Bladebreakers were World Champions! It was amazing! Everybody couldn't wait to take me on!

So What's Next?

You didn't really think that the Bladebreakers were through, did you? We make a great team! And it sure looks like we have our work cut out for us. We may be the defending champs, but once again, there's much more at stake than winning a trophy. This time we seem to be on the most-wanted list of a whole new crew of bad guys — and they're after our Bit Beasts, too! What's up with these people?!

But worse than any of that is the possibility that one of the Bladebreakers has betrayed us! Who is it? Well, you'll just have to stay tuned to find out.

Get ready to feel the force!

BEYBLADE: THE SPORT

How to Be a Beyblade Champion

So now that you know all about our Beyblade adventures, you'd probably like some advice from the pros, right? Well, my best advice is to practice, practice, practice! If you want to be a winner, then you have to realize that there's always room for improvement, and it takes a lot of dedication and hard work to be the best. Of course, you also need to know the basics, and that's what I'm going to help you out with here.

What Is Beyblade?

It's the best sport around! Beyblade is played using the next generation of high-performance spinning tops. Players send their Beyblades spinning into a Beystadium

56

and fiercely battle it out for the win. How you win depends on the rules you're playing with, but what you usually want to do is either knock your opponent's blade out of the battle, or outlast it and remain spinning after it has stopped.

Beyblade has really taken off in the past few years, and the BBA is stepping up its tournament action. For more information about Beyblade tournaments in your area, go to www.beyblade.com. But you don't have to wait for the BBA — you can hold your own battles. The more you play, the more experience you get, so it makes sense to practice hard and play often. If you are looking for more people who share your interest, there are also Beyblade groups online. If you join a group, you can find great information on customizing your Beyblade, pick up some new battle tips and meet other bladers like you.

When you're online, never give out any personal information. Don't share your full name and address, and be careful what you tell people about yourself.

The Blades

There are many different Beyblades available. Some are easily found, while others are much more rare — they're limited editions. Before you buy a Beyblade, you might want to consider your personality and think about what your fighting style might be like. Are you looking for an Attack Type blade, a Defense Type blade, an Endurance Type blade, or a Combination Type blade? Do some research, so you'll have a good idea of which blade is right for you.

There's lots of information online, and you can look at the back of the boxes that Beyblades come in. There you can find the blade's Attack/Defense/Endurance Stats that will tell you what it's been designed for.

Most bladers will tell you that the key to their success has been their customized blades. These bladers take individual parts from the different blades they've bought or traded, and then they create their own customized blades. Many people have combinations that they think work the best, but you should try a number of your own customizations and see which one works the best for you — everybody's different!

The Right Five Pieces Equal a Winning Blade

There are five parts to a Beyblade, and each part is interchangeable with similar parts from another blade. Each part plays an important role in determining your blade's fighting style, so it's important to understand how they work.

1. The Bit Chip — this tells you about the blade's spirit. You don't need this piece to make the blade work, but many bladers prefer to have it. They believe it represents their fighting spirit and could even contain a powerful Bit Beast.

2. The Attack Ring — this determines the blade's attack strength and type. It is the widest part of the Beyblade, and, depending on its shape, it can act offensively or defensively. The Attack Ring is the first part of your Beyblade to make contact with your opponent's Beyblade. Check out the Stat rating on the box. A ring with a high Attack Stat will behave much more offensively than one with a lower Attack Stat.

3. The Weight Disk — this sets a blade's strength and endurance. A heavy Weight Disk might increase a blade's strength and stamina, but a light one allows for more movement. You'll have to decide which one you prefer!

4. The Spin Gear — this determines the blade's spin direction. Most Spin Gears cause the blade to spin clockwise, or to the right, but some Beyblades have spin gears that can spin counterclockwise, or to the left. If you change the spin of your blade, you should remember that it will really change how your Attack Ring works.

5. The Blade Base — this piece is responsible for the blade's movement patterns and the height of the Beyblade. A Blade Base with a flat base, or a high grip tip, will cause the blade to circle around in the dish far more than one with a pointy tip. This is the only part of your blade that you want to come in contact with the stadium!

What Are All Those Stars Doing on the Side of the Box?

When you buy a new Beyblade, you'll notice the Stat Chart on the side of its box. This chart tells you how the Attack Ring, the Weight Disk and the Blade Base are rated in terms of their Attack ability, their Defense ability and their Endurance ability. You can choose the blade that's right for you based on these stats. If you want a more aggressive style, you're obviously going to look for pieces that have a high Attack stat. The same is true for blades that are better at defense and endurance.

The box also has a label telling you how the Beyblade it contains performs as a whole. It will be labelled as an Attack Type, Defense Type, Endurance Type or Combination Type — meaning it has all-around decent ratings in Attack, Defense and Endurance. That way you make sure you get the blade that best matches your fighting style.

The All-Important Beystadium!

Each Beystadium has its own unique design, with different challenges. Right now the biggest difference between basic Beystadiums is the slope of their walls, but there are a few advanced stadiums with special features, and more are in development all the time.

The Launcher and Ripcord

How you launch your Beyblade is just as important as the type of Beyblade you're using. You want to make sure that your launcher is in really good working order and that you've perfected your pulling technique. If you look on the launcher, there's a small diagram that shows you the right way to put the ripcord in. The launcher locks on to your blade, and once you've pulled the cord through it, the spin stops and it locks, releasing your blade. Any real blader will tell you that your success in battle depends a lot on how well you've launched your blade, and your launch technique, so this is something you'll want to practice quite often. You should hold your launcher as steady as possible, and pull the cord away from your body with as much force as you can — the faster the better. Some bladers suggest that you try pulling the launcher along the ripcord, and that's something that you can try too. In fact, you should try as many different ways of launching your blade that you can think of. You can also upgrade your basic launcher, or get an advanced launcher or shooter. These can offer better grips, a sighting scope and the ability to measure your rip speed. Some launchers even allow you to fight virtual opponents that you see on the shooter's display!

Beyblade Basic Rules of Play

These are great standard rules to follow when you're not battling in a BBA tournament.

1. All Beyblade battles must occur in a Beystadium! A Beystadium cannot be on a table or other elevated surface. Warning: never lean over a Beystadium while the blades inside are still spinning!

2. To begin official Beyblade battles, Beyblade tops must be launched after the signal of "3, 2, 1 LET IT RIP!"

3. Only one launch per battle — the battle ends when there is only one top left spinning.

4. If player touches opponent during opponent's launch of top, player loses 1 point.

5. Player scores 1 point if opponent does not launch top into the Beystadium.

6. If player's top enters one of the three penalty pockets anytime during battle, opponent scores 2 points (max score of 2 points per battle).

7. Player scores 1 point if his or her top spins longer than opponent's top.

8. If player touches Beystadium during battle, opponent scores 3 points, and the battle is immediately over.

9. Compete in multiple battles — the player with 7 or more points at the completion of a battle wins!

Special Power Spirit Rules for More Extreme Beyblade Action!

Each battle is fought under one special rule of play. Will your opponent change his battle strategy? Can you use the rule to your advantage? LET IT RIP and find out!

1. Dragoon Storm (Dragon Spirit) Reverse Launch = Opponent must launch his/her top with his/her opposite (non-writing) hand.

2. Draciel (Turtle Spirit) Delay Launch = Launch your Beyblade top 5 seconds after opponent launches his/her top.

3. Dranzer (Phoenix Spirit) Power Launch = Player can use a Deluxe Beyblade launcher while opponent can only use the standard Beyblade launcher.

4. Driger (White Tiger Spirit) Customization Launch = Opponent cannot use a customized top. His/her top must come straight out of the box.

5. Why not come up with your own great Spirit Rule?

Don't Let it Stop Here!

There are many different ways to battle, so for fun you can try playing with different rules. I know you've seen the Bladebreakers in free-for-all matches — that's when a group of people throw their blades in together and the last blade standing wins. But a lot of the time our matches are the best two out of three. You can play this way as a team, by selecting three players, or you can try this as an individual, by using three different blades.

Beyblade Battle Association Official Rules of Play

These are the rules you will need to know if you plan on entering a BBA Tournament.

1. A BATTLE will consist of 2 Competitors launching their tops into BEYSTADIUM upon the REFEREE's call of "3,2,1 LET IT RIP!"

2. The BATTLE ends when one top stops spinning.

3. Only one launch is allowed per BATTLE.

4. Each ROUND will consist of 3 BATTLES.

5. If it is determined by the REFEREE that both of the BEYBLADE tops stop spinning at the same time the BATTLE will be declared a TIE.

6. Each Competitor will compete in ROUND 1. Competitors who win the ROUND will move to the next ROUND. Competitors who lose the ROUND will be eliminated from the competition.

7. The Winner of the ROUND will be the Competitor who wins the majority of the 3 BATTLES — either by winning 2 of the 3 BATTLES or by winning 1 BATTLE when the other 2 BATTLES are considered a TIE.

8. If a ROUND ends with 3 TIE BATTLES, additional BATTLES will be played until a BATTLE is won. The winner of that BATTLE will be declared the winner of that ROUND.

9. All BEYBLADE BATTLES will occur in a BEYSTADIUM.

10. Semi-Final and Final ROUNDS will occur in the Official BBA BEYBLADE Competition Stadiums.

11. BEYBLADE tops must be launched immediately following the signal "3, 2, 1 LET IT RIP!"

12. Competitors who launch their tops prior to the signal of "3,2,1 LET IT RIP!" will automatically lose that BATTLE.

13. Competitors who delay the launch of their tops beyond the signal of "3, 2, 1 LET IT RIP!" will automatically lose that BATTLE.

14. If a Competitor touches his or her Opponent or the Beystadium during the BATTLE, he or she will automatically lose that BATTLE.

15. Competitors must launch their tops from within the designated area.

16. Competitors cannot launch their tops from a standing, jumping or running position.

17. If a Competitor is not present at the beginning of the BATTLE, then the Opponent will automatically win by default.

18. It is the Competitor's responsibility to be present at their assigned BEYSTADIUM with a working top, launcher and rip cord at the pre-determined time.

19. If a top enters a side pocket in the BEYSTADIUM and continues to spin longer than the Opponent's top it will be declared the winner.

20. If at any time during the BATTLE a top launches outside the BEYSTADIUM it will be disqualified and the Opponent will automatically be declared the winner of that BATTLE.

21. Only Official BEYBLADE tops, Stadiums, Rip Cords and Launchers manufactured by Hasbro are eligible for Official BBA tournament play.

22. Hasbro-manufactured "Electronic Tops" are not allowed for Official BBA Tournament play.

23. Each BEYBLADE top must contain a minimum of: Attack Ring, Weight Disk, Spin Gear and Blade Base manufactured by Hasbro to be eligible for Official BBA Tournament Play. The use of the Bit is optional.

24. If a Competitor is found to be using a non-Official top he or she will only be allowed to continue in the tournament by using an Official BEYBLADE.

25. If a Competitor suspects an Opponent is using a non-Official top it is his or her responsibility to communicate this to the REFEREE.

26. All tops must be assembled and ready for battle once the Competitors enter the tournament area. Competitors are not allowed to reconfigure their tops during the ROUND.

27. If a Competitor is not prepared when the BATTLE begins he or she will forfeit the BATTLE and his or her Opponent will win by default.

28. If a REFEREE requests the inspection of a BEYBLADE top, the player has to disassemble the BEYBLADE and accept immediate inspection.

29. BEYBLADE tops that do not disassemble are not allowed for Official BBA Tournament play.

30. The use of modified or broken BEYBLADE parts is prohibited. If parts are found to be broken, worn out or purposely modified they must be replaced immediately.

31. Competitors must ensure their BEYBLADE tops are properly assembled prior to battle.

32. It is prohibited to purposely launch a BEYBLADE at a person at any time.

33. A Competitor can be ejected from the tournament if the Competitor violates regulations and/or performs in an unsportsmanlike manner.

34. Rules are subject to change without notice.

35. All decisions of the REFEREES regarding these Rules are final.

So What's the One Thing You Can Do to Become a Championship Beyblader?

PRACTICE! You need to practice with different blade configurations until you find the parts that work best together. Keep a record of how each configuration performed, and try exchanging one piece at a time until you find the combination that gives you what you're looking for.

Practice your launch. Like I said before, try lots of different techniques — some people move the launcher along the ripcord, others practice pulling the ripcord through the launcher as fast and smoothly as possible. You can see what happens when you hold the launcher at different angles, from different heights.

Practice your aim. Try aiming at a stable target that you've placed within the Beystadium. Can you hit it every time?

Practice your battle technique. You can practice on your own, but battling other bladers gives you a broader range of experience.

That's it.

That's the key to being a championship Beyblader: lots of hard work and determination. Just don't forget why you started playing it in the first place — to have fun!

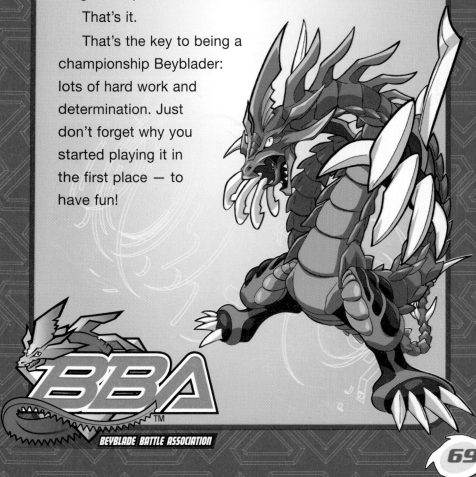

BBA™

BEYBLADE BATTLE ASSOCIATION

*T*here you have it — everything you need
to know about Beyblade!
But don't forget to watch us defend
our World Championship title
in *Beyblade II, VForce!*
The action will be even fiercer than before,
and there's a whole new crew of baddies —
like Team Psykick and the Saint Shields!
So tune in, and don't forget to . . .

LET IT RIP!